A DORLING KINDERSLEY BOOK

First published in Great Britain in 1992
by Dorling Kindersley Limited,
9 Henrietta Street, London WC2E 8PS
Copyright © 1992 Dorling Kindersley Limited, London
Reprinted in 1992

For Sam

A CIP catalogue record for this book is
available from the British Library
ISBN 0-86318-970-9

Colour reproduction by Dot Gradations
Printed and bound by L.E.G.O. in Vicenza, Italy

Wrinkly ANIMALS

Illustrated by
Kenneth Lilly

Written by
Angela Wilkes

DORLING KINDERSLEY
London • New York • Stuttgart

Contents

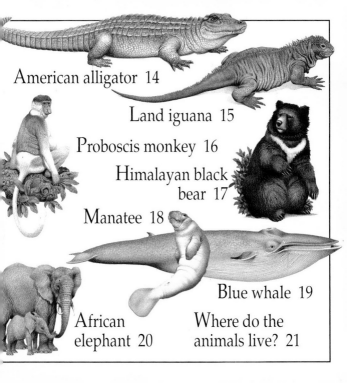

Elephant seal
The seal's thick skin
and layers of fat help
it to keep warm
in icy seas.

Andean condor
This vulture is
one of the biggest
flying birds ever
to have lived.

9

Rhinoceros
The rhinoceros's thick, leathery skin
hangs in folds, making it look baggy.

10

Hippopotamus

The hippopotamus spends most of
the day wallowing in water, or
lounging on sand banks.

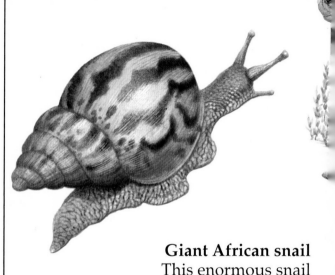

Giant African snail
This enormous snail
slithers through the rainforest,
eating all kinds of plants.

12

Giant tortoise
The tortoise can
tuck its head
and legs into its
shell for protection.

13

American alligator
This fierce-looking alligator digs
deep holes in the swamps
where it lives.

Land iguana
This wrinkled lizard eats nothing but plants. It even eats prickly cacti!

15

Proboscis monkey
The male monkey has a large nose that he uses to call loudly, warning other monkeys of danger.

16

Himalayan black bear
This chubby bear eats a lot in autumn, then sleeps all winter when food is hard to find.

17

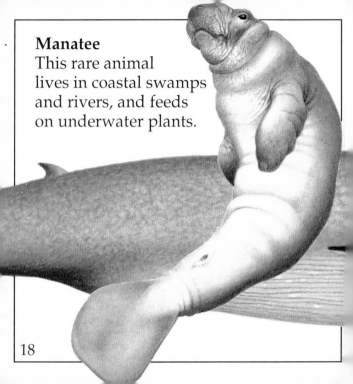

Manatee
This rare animal lives in coastal swamps and rivers, and feeds on underwater plants.

18

Blue whale
The blue whale is the largest living
animal and swims in cold seas.

19

African elephant
Even baby elephants have thick, tough
skin that looks old and wrinkled.

Where do the animals live?

Elephant seal
Southern Seas

Andean condor
Andes, South America

Rhinoceros
African grasslands

Hippopotamus
African rivers

Giant African snail
African rainforests

Giant tortoise
Galapagos Islands

American alligator
The Everglades,
North America

Land iguana
Galapagos Islands

Proboscis monkey
South East Asia

Himalayan black bear
The Himalayas

Manatee
Warm coasts of Africa
and North America

Blue whale
Cold seas

African elephant
African grasslands

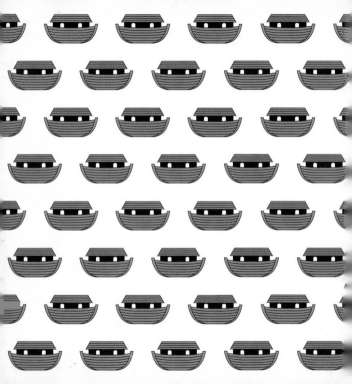